Tiptoe Into SCARY PLACES

HORROR HOTELS

by Kathryn Camisa

Consultant: Ursula Bielski
Author and Paranormal Researcher
Founder of Chicago Hauntings, Inc.

BEARPORT
PUBLISHING

New York, New York

Credits

Cover, © Stepstock/Fotolia; TOC, © Sean Pavone/iStock; 4–5, © ggustin/iStock, © Graeme Dawes/Shutterstock, © Hans-Juergen Luntzer/Shutterstock, © Olaf Naami/Shutterstock, © Lario Tus/Shutterstock, and © Michael Dechev/Shutterstock; 6L, © laura.h/Shutterstock; 6R, © Yuguesh Fagoonee/Shutterstock; 7, © Nate Allred/Shutterstock; 8–9, © bonetta/iStock; 9R, © ValaGrenier/iStock; 10, © Jim Barber/Shutterstock; 11, © Sponner/Shutterstock; 12, © Jeff Thrower/Shutterstock; 13, © Peter Dedeurwaerder/Shutterstock; 14, © Nick Kenrick/Flickr/cc BY 2.0; 15, © Vintage Images/Alamy; 16, © alfocome/Shutterstock; 17, © Nadya Lukic/Shutterstock; 18, © Peter Hess; 19, © The Miriam and Ira D. Wallach Division of Art, Prints and Photographs: Photography Collection, The New York Public Library; 20, © Peter Newark Military Pictures/Bridgeman Images; 21, © jdwfoto/Shutterstock; 23, © Svetlana Eremina/Shutterstock; 24, © Dave Kotinsky/Shutterstock.

Publisher: Kenn Goin
Senior Editor: Joyce Tavolacci
Creative Director: Spencer Brinker
Photo Researcher: Thomas Persano
Cover: Kim Jones

Library of Congress Cataloging-in-Publication Data

Names: Camisa, Kathryn, author.
Title: Horror hotels / by Kathryn Camisa.
Description: New York : Bearport Publishing Company, Inc., 2017. | Series: Tiptoe into scary places | Includes bibliographical references and index.
Identifiers: LCCN 2016042370 (print) | LCCN 2016044437 (ebook) | ISBN 9781684020461 (library) | ISBN 9781684020980 (ebook)
Subjects: LCSH: Haunted hotels—Juvenile literature.
Classification: LCC BF1474.5 .C36 2017 (print) | LCC BF1474.5 (ebook) | DDC 133.1/2—dc23
LC record available at https://lccn.loc.gov/2016042370

For more information, write to Bearport Publishing Company, Inc., 45 West 21st Street, Suite 3B, New York, New York 10010. Printed in the United States of America.

10 9 8 7 6 5 4 3 2 1

CONTENTS

HORROR HOTELS

You've just placed your head on a pillow and closed your eyes. An icy breeze **grazes** your neck. Suddenly, the floor creaks. You hear footsteps beside your bed. Your hands shake as you slowly turn on a light. Then you realize you're the only person in the hotel room!

DANGER
KEEP OUT

Get ready to read four chilling tales about haunted hotels. Turn the page . . . if you have the nerve!

5

THE GHOST BRIDE

The Fairmont Banff Springs Hotel, Banff, Canada

A wedding day is often one of the happiest days of a bride's life. Sadly, for one bride, it was also her last.

It was the early 1930s at the Fairmont Hotel. The bride climbed the hotel's large staircase. Candles lit her way. She was eager to dance with her new husband.

The Fairmont Banff Springs Hotel

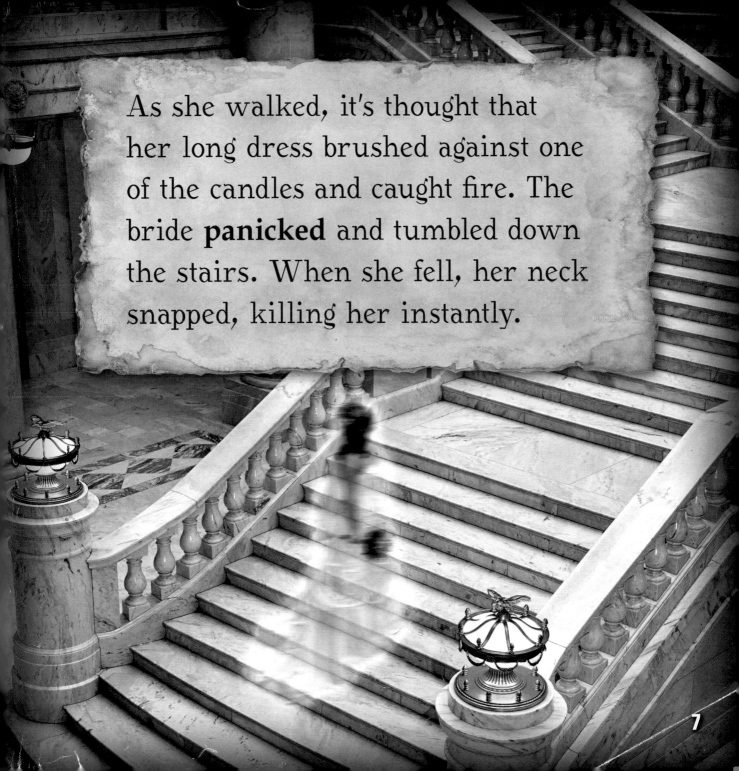

As she walked, it's thought that her long dress brushed against one of the candles and caught fire. The bride **panicked** and tumbled down the stairs. When she fell, her neck snapped, killing her instantly.

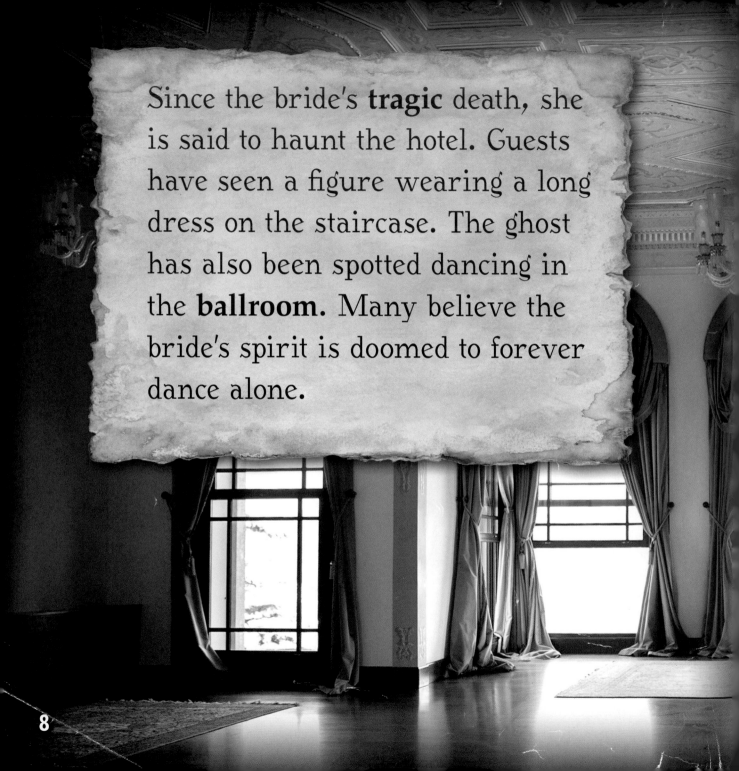

Since the bride's **tragic** death, she is said to haunt the hotel. Guests have seen a figure wearing a long dress on the staircase. The ghost has also been spotted dancing in the **ballroom.** Many believe the bride's spirit is doomed to forever dance alone.

Hotel guests have also seen a veiled figure wandering the halls near where the bride died.

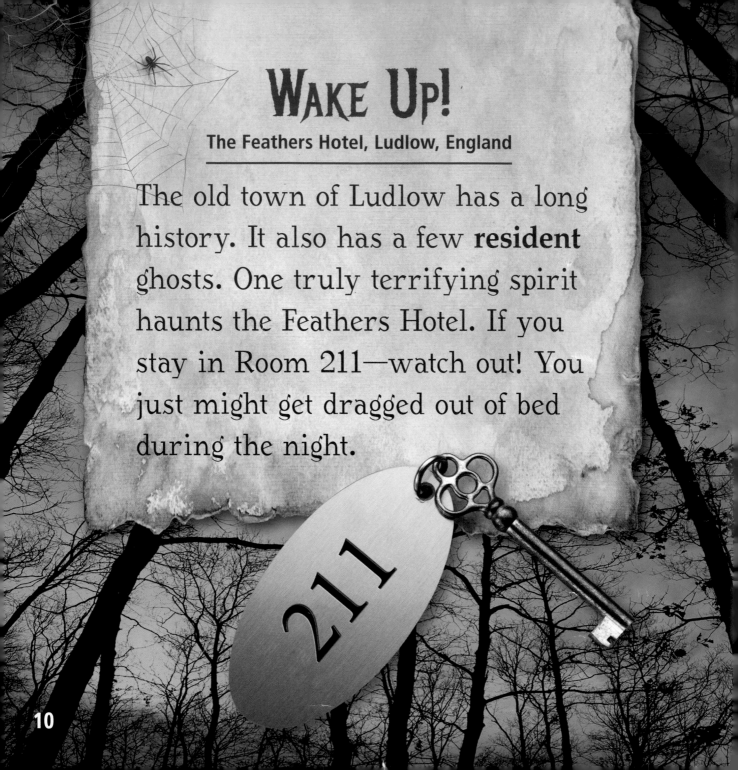

WAKE UP!

The Feathers Hotel, Ludlow, England

The old town of Ludlow has a long history. It also has a few **resident** ghosts. One truly terrifying spirit haunts the Feathers Hotel. If you stay in Room 211—watch out! You just might get dragged out of bed during the night.

211

The Feathers Hotel was built in 1619.

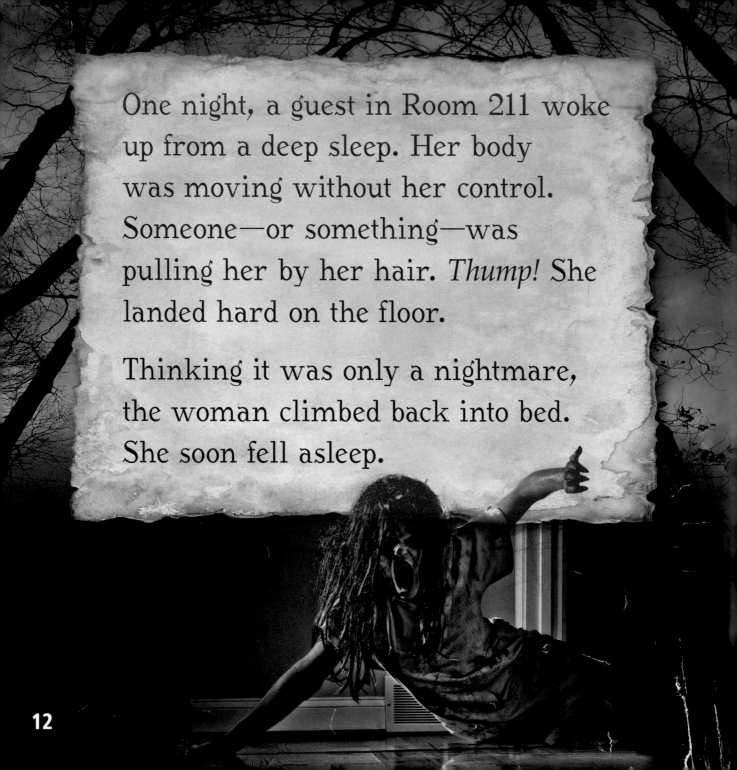

One night, a guest in Room 211 woke up from a deep sleep. Her body was moving without her control. Someone—or something—was pulling her by her hair. *Thump!* She landed hard on the floor.

Thinking it was only a nightmare, the woman climbed back into bed. She soon fell asleep.

In the morning, the woman awoke shivering. Her nightgown was soaked with water. Had the terrifying ghost returned in the night to **taunt** her?

The ghosts of a man and a dog have also been spotted at the hotel. They have been seen walking from Room 232 into Room 233. Then they disappear!

Friend or Foe?

The Savoy Hotel, Mussoorie, India

The Savoy Hotel in India is home to a ghostly visitor. Who is the spooky guest? The tragic story of Lady Frances Garnett-Orme may hold the answer.

The Savoy Hotel

Early one morning, Lady Frances was found dead in her hotel room. Police were called to the scene. They saw no signs of a break-in. Who had killed the poor woman?

A doctor later discovered that poison had been added to one of Lady Frances's medicine bottles. She had been murdered!

It's said that a ghost has haunted the hotel ever since. A lady in white has been seen wandering the hallways. The spirit has approached guests, **gazed** into their eyes, and then **vanished.** Many believe Lady Frances's ghost is looking for her killer.

Eva Montstephen, Lady Frances's friend, was **arrested** for the murder.

THE HEADLESS BODY

The Battery Carriage House Inn, Charleston, South Carolina

Charleston has a long and bloody past. Many **Civil War** battles took place in the city. Lots of young soldiers lost their lives. It's no wonder that restless spirits roam the city. At the Battery Carriage House Inn, visitors might even wake up next to one!

The Battery Carriage House Inn

The destroyed city of Charleston after the Civil War

19

One night, a guest at the inn was jolted awake. He saw shadows dancing around his room. Then, right before his eyes, he saw the outline of a body beside him in bed!

The man's hand reached out to touch the **torso**. That's when he saw that the body didn't have a head or face! Then the body let out a

The headless ghost is believed to be a long dead Civil War soldier.

horrifying growling sound. Stunned,
the man screamed. He turned on the
light. Yet all he saw was an empty bed.

HORROR HOTELS
AROUND THE WORLD

THE FAIRMONT BANFF SPRINGS HOTEL
Banff, Canada

Discover the place where a young bride died on her wedding day.

THE BATTERY CARRIAGE HOUSE INN
Charleston, South Carolina

Explore one of America's most haunted inns!

THE FEATHERS HOTEL
Ludlow, England

Check out a hotel room that is home to a very unfriendly ghost.

THE SAVOY HOTEL
Mussoorie, India

Visit the hotel where a woman's ghost still searches for her killer!

Arctic Ocean

NORTH AMERICA

Atlantic Ocean

EUROPE

ASIA

Pacific Ocean

AFRICA

Pacific Ocean

SOUTH AMERICA

Atlantic Ocean

Indian Ocean

AUSTRALIA

N
W E
S

Southern Ocean

ANTARCTICA

Glossary

arrested (uh-REST-id) seized by police

ballroom (BAWL-*room*) a very large room where parties and dances are held

Civil War (SIV-il WOR) the U.S. War between the Northern states and the Southern states, which lasted from 1861 to 1865

gazed (GAYZD) stared at something

grazes (GRAYZ-iz) brushes lightly

panicked (PAN-ikt) filled with fear

resident (REZ-uh-duhnt) a person who lives in a particular place

taunt (TAWNT) to try to make someone upset

torso (TOR-soh) the part of the body between a person's neck and waist, not including the arms

tragic (TRAJ-ik) very sad or unfortunate

vanished (VAN-ishd) disappeared suddenly from sight

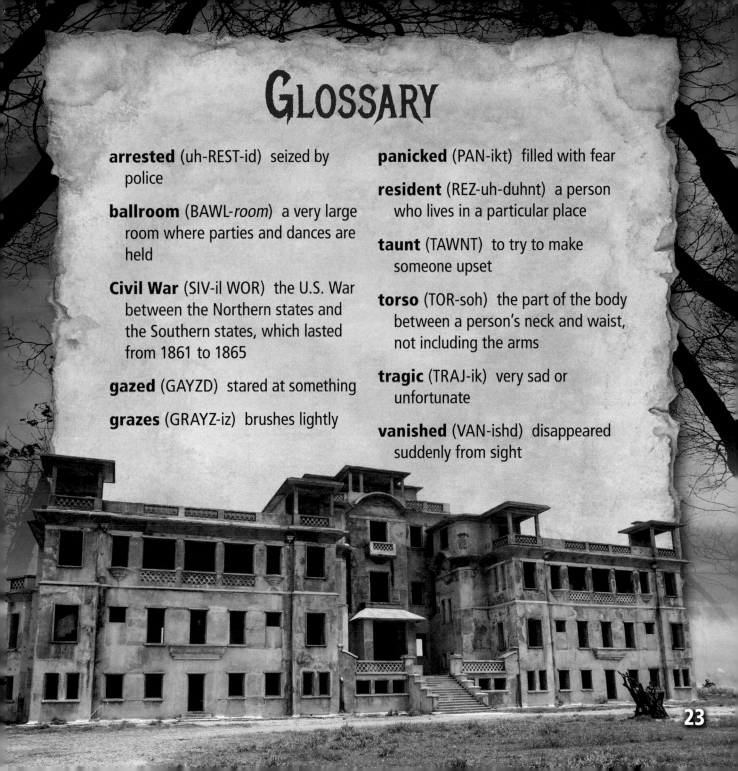

Index

Read More

Penn-Coughin, O. *They're Coming For You: Scary Stories That Scream to be Read.* New York: CreateSpace (2011).

Phillips, Dee. *The Deadly Secret of Room 213 (Cold Whispers II).* New York: Bearport (2017).

Learn More Online

To learn more about horror hotels, visit:
www.bearportpublishing.com/Tiptoe

About the Author

Kathryn Camisa once stayed at a castle believed to be haunted. Unfortunately, she did not meet any ghosts during her visit.